Create Your Own Business Cash Flow Fountain

LEGAL NOTICES

The information presented herein represents the view of the authors as of the date of publication. Because of the rate with which conditions change, the author reserves the right to alter and update his opinion based on the new conditions. This book is for informational purposes only. While every attempt has been made to verify the information provided in this book, neither the authors nor their affiliates/partners assume any responsibility for errors, inaccuracies or omissions. Any slights of people or organizations are unintentional. You should be aware of any laws which govern business transactions or other business practices in your country and state. Any reference to any person or business whether living or dead is purely coincidental.

Every effort has been made to accurately represent this product and it's potential. Examples in these materials are not to be interpreted as a promise or guarantee of earnings. Earning potential is entirely dependent on the person using our product, ideas and techniques. We do not purport this as a "get rich scheme."

Your level of success in attaining the results claimed in our materials depends on the time you devote to the program, ideas and techniques mentioned your finances, knowledge and various skills. Since these factors differ according to individuals, we cannot guarantee your success or income level. Nor are we responsible for any of your actions.

Any and all forward looking statements here or on any of our sales material are intended to express our opinion of earnings potential. Many factors will be important in determining your actual results and no guarantees are made that you will achieve results similar to ours or anybody else's, in fact no guarantees are made that you will achieve any results from our ideas and techniques in our material.

ALL RIGHTS RESERVED. No part of this course may be reproduced or transmitted in any form whatsoever, electronic, or mechanical, including photocopying, recording, or by any informational storage or retrieval without the expressed written consent of the authors.

Create Your Own Business Cash Flow Fountain

Create Your Own Cash Rich Business, Implement Transformational Marketing Strategies And Enjoy Year Round, Market Beating Performance!

Stuart Bowker

"I keep getting jewels of wisdom"

Kane Yeardley, Forum Bars Group

Do You Want a Transformation?

So you want to either build a new business that has market beating cash flow, or add that extra something that transforms the cash flow of the business you already have?

- Do you want to stay up to date with the marketing that is working right now, the activity that keeps you ahead of the competition in a market that seems to be driven by price? Do you want to avoid making the BIG mistake that puts you and your prosperity under pressure?

- I know you want to eliminate the guess work in targeting your ideal customers, and enable you to have predictable, and repeatable performance!

- Look "Behind the Curtain" at the things the most admired operators are implementing to keep their business cash rich and super lean. These insights keep more money in your pocket to spend on what YOU want to, when YOU want to!

- Do you want to build a "System and Resource Centre" that you can go back to and use, eliminating the guess work and helping you Earn More and Work Less?

For your gateway access to all of this and a FREE assessment of a current piece of your marketing plan, worth £200, join me at the social media page at KingsOfCashflow.com

Stuart@KingsOfCashflow.com

TABLE OF CONTENTS

PART ONE: Why Build the Fountain?

PART TWO: Turning On The Taps

PART THREE: Making the Decisions

PART FOUR: Success Path

INTRODUCTION

Who the Hell is Stuart Bowker...and why the heck should I listen to a word he says? How can he help me build a business cash flow fountain, help me achieve my goals and stop trading my time for money?

Here's my story, the first thing you should know about me is that I'm not a business guru who has not worked with "hands-on" real experience.

I don't hold an MBA or lots of qualifications for the sake of being an "expert". In fact the only thing I consider myself an expert in is understanding systems, improving on them and enabling others to get the most out of them for transformational results.

Mostly for the benefit of their business, often for their own knowledge and understanding in its own right.

I have worked at the "front line" dealing with customers directly and had the benefit of working in fast moving customer led businesses. I do have 20 years of working with multiple and varied businesses across the country delivering results for big companies and owner operators alike.

The Cash Flow Fountain is a system put together through pure necessity. Finding myself unexpectedly with a lack of financial freedom and an income that reduced the choices I had for myself and a young family I learnt through mistakes, trial and error but mostly a willingness to implement and improve systems to get the full benefit of my trading my effort for profit, *not time for money.*

Are you tired of the LACK of financial freedom and limited choices that operating your business in its current format brings?

Let's be honest if you have been in business for 1 year or 10, standing on the side lines with trepidation about starting a venture, the **KEY** to unlocking the potential is being able to turn on reliable cash flow performance like a tap that becomes a fountain.

The economy in the news is apparently improving, depending on what flavour of politics you prefer we are either being hoodwinked or on our way to Babylon by bus....the National Minimum Wage is brilliant for some or known as "National Price Hike Day" to cover the difference....the cost of living increases and people are at the mercy of big businesses that control our commodities.

Your OPPORTUNITIES ARE REDUCING

Maybe you have seen your apparently loyal customers go to your competition chasing a better price, even sometimes offers you can see must be making NO MONEY for the rivals, but they now have your customer.

Your customers are experiencing the cash flow issues that you can insulate yourself against in both the short and long term. If history has taught us anything it's that the market place when things get tough starts to get more and more brutal, relationships matter less and the offer that is available matters more. CASH is KING and if you have more of it in the deal you have more choices available to make better decisions in both acquiring customers and moving your business forwards.

When CASH FLOW is strong you can ensure that your business grows, you can retain your customers and you can implement transformational plans and systems that make your business bomb-proof in these testing times.

As you consider how different your life would be with a business that spins off cash that you can decide what you want to spend it on, rather than wondering if the business will get through another month, you realise that it's the CASH FLOW that needs to improve.

You can imagine the change in your outlook, the great feeling that comes with **knowing** that you can turn on the taps to the fountain when you want and that the results are, MEASURABLE, PREDICTABLE AND REPEATABLE.

Of course there may be things holding you back, it could be the time to learn how, knowing which things work rather than relying on luck or chance. You would like to take a decision that you can rely on from a proven track record and probably assume that some of the "edge" that people have on you is a secret system, method or blueprint that they have....

Systems Always Win….

You know that these "secrets" just need to be pulled together and you get the look behind the curtain that will ensure your chances of making errors and costing you money are addressed, secrets that if someone can draw them out for you are going to make a BIG difference to your future freedom and success.

You have made the right decision when you picked up your copy of this book, because as you turn the pages you will realise how you can take the guess work out of what you want to achieve, AND realise how you can turn the odds your way. How you can create your cash rich business, implement bombproof marketing strategies and enjoy year round, market beating performance!

This book is dramatically different from anything you have read- by a mile- it will give you a multi-faceted outlook, **showing you** what to do, **guiding you** through **making it happen** and leaving you with a transformational action plan at the end- a plan you can return to time and again.

At just 100 pages or so it's content rich and you can read it through in an afternoon, go back to it after that and implement in less than 30 days the transformational action sheets to secure your own;

Profit Producing Machine

Turbo charge your performance and own your part of what might be a tough market place but one that's plenty big enough to accommodate your CASH FLOW FOUNTAIN.

Your first step now is to get stuck in, you can silence the doubts in your mind and appreciate that the "secrets" are being revealed for you to make the difference to your own goals and the financial choices that you and your family have available to you.

To your success!

Stuart Bowker

If you are looking for resources that after you have read this book you can implement to transform your business, you can keep up to date with myself and what is working right now by following the link below;

www.KingsOfCashflow.com
Email: Stuart@KingsofCashflow.com

PART ONE:

WHY BUILD THE FOUNTAIN?

What's Your Vision?

There needs to be a vision for where you are going, although it sounds back to front, knowing how you are going to sell your product or service **before** you identify the solution you are going to offer the market is key.

Knowing this will allow you to make sound decisions on the costs of the product, service and marketing so that it delivers to the market place with cash flow capability still intact.

A vision of what you are trying to achieve, not just based on "earn more money", that keeps you engaged in the business and the long term satisfied customers is also a sound point to cover for your own motivation to consistently get the job done.

When you start with a system in mind and build the business from the ground up, underpinning what you do, in a fairly short period of time you will become more time efficient and more effective.

Your system will present to you what works and what does not. This system will also mean that you have standard forms potentially for making things happen, this is all time saved, with a system you can also hand this work on to others and buy yourself back the time to market and develop the business.

Where Are We Going?

I know you want to build a business that throws off cash from the beginning, a guide that takes you through a long plan would not work, this gets straight to the nitty gritty! This is distilled down to the core ideas that you need to action quickly- this will shape up over 30 days, a day to absorb the info a day to implement.

You want to start building your business and tap into the Cash Flow Fountain NOW! All this guide does is show you this...I'd suggest that you think that this is a boiled down- results focused plan to get you rocking and rolling....take action and implement, if you need to find someone to do some work for you (virtual PA, accountants) then do that- you need a mindset that you are an entrepreneur.

That is your focus, **you are going to build your cash flow** and have money to spend on what you want and reinvest in growing the business.

Cash flow is the life blood of any business, without it you can't make progress and the business you create will not keep you motivated to keep at it.

Over my 20 years of involvement with many businesses, I know that this is the area that when you get it right- **and you will**- it can really change the dynamic of the business you have, or when it is a new business get it off on the right foot to spin off cash for you.

One of businesses I have worked with had two premises- both country pubs- the toughest time of year was January when everyone is short of leisure spending money and are watching their waist lines.

The sole reason it was the toughest time of year was cash flow. This lack of cash flow killed profit, stopped marketing activity, presented the risk of short term credit terms being required and in the end just caused stress.

A Business Cash Flow Fountain needed turning on!

One simple marketing activity that I identified and recommended, was focused, and delivered an irresistible offer directly to his already happy customers. The cash flow change ensured that January was a profitable month, so much so that the pub profit was up 5000%!

May have been a small base to work from but the Return on Investment (ROI) on £150 spent was phenomenal. In addition he gathered more information about his customers to turn on this Fountain of Cash Flow -as a system- again in the future. The secret? He **implemented** the plan.

Getting Started

There are so many people who say they want to start or build their own business, but don't seem to get around to it at the time for loads of reasons- a lot of those people like to talk about it rather than take the action that makes the BIG difference to their lives and their business success.

In fact you can start and build a business now faster than you have ever have been able to before.

If you are reading this you are an action taker, next step is to be a super implementer to ensure that the effort you put in gives the result you are after, the two need to happen hand in hand. I am going to walk you through the decision making process that will, with your implementation, guide you to the points that will lead you to be successful.

This can be done cheaper than ever before. You may want to be running a business alongside your regular job or get to a point where you can use the income from the business to produce cash that replaces your regular income, the extra money you can spend for you, not something that becomes a merry-go-round that only buys you another job.

Good cash flow coupled with a strong grip on your return on investment numbers will deliver the financial goals that you set yourself.

Building a Business Cash Flow Fountain will enable you to set a blue print that you can either apply to the business you have now or set up your first cash producing business. The methods will ensure that you have enough money to be able to buy yourself choices.

This cash is what you can spend on experiences you can remember with your loved ones or, if your thing is luxury items then they are in reach.

As you progress with this plan and implement to build your business, there are things you can do for yourself to go to another level. Become part of local business networks, find an "accountability partner" who will help you deliver on the promises you make to yourself and your business progress.

There are also opportunities to join the Kings Of Cashflow Inner Circle where you can share in the ideas and plans that will continue your momentum and success. Just go to KingsofCashflow.com

Set the Date!

So this is a 30 day implementer's plan- 15 days of action plan, with 15 days in there to put it into practice. Take each of the steps yourself (even if this is arranging someone to take the load off your desk). Set the date now on this page, set the date now on your notice board, a white board, on your phone front screen- which date? 30 days from NOW!

You want to hold yourself to account, set yourself a target that ensures that you follow through and deliver on the promise to yourself. Cash flow comes from implementing, you want to have an impact on your wallet you need to do something about it.

Sounds a bit "out there", but giving this your focus, setting a date and becoming an expert in a short time on taking the right actions is what will make the activity pay off- *and that's what we both want. WHAT GETS MEASURED GETS DONE….*

Today's Date	
Implementers Date	

This activity will be transformational for any current business you have, and ensure that you have a fast route to cash flow success in any new business venture.

Systems Win

McDonalds DON'T have the best burgers, there I've said it! What they are great at though is having systems, they have a system for turning on equipment to best effect for customer demand, cleaning regimes and their heating bills.

This is why the main menu is only available after 10.30 in the morning. This system is written down in an operations manual, there are support documents and notices to make it work with a team that may be quite new. The customers know they cannot buy the main menu before 10.30, they have been "trained" by the company.

This system means that McDonalds can sell their whole operating system to new franchisees, these franchisees follow the manual, understand how the parent company works and how they squeeze the pips for profit. McDonalds can then build the company to be the world wide success it is.

Not the best burger, but the best system to deliver the most burgers with the best profitability, to the most people. They know the customer needs and answer that with best effect. Burger King may be better but the delivery misses the mark for the customer needs. The system wins.

Have in your mind from here on, what will you be able to systemise? How do you set up your system that you can sell later or have others run it when you are not there?

Why Do YOU Want it?

Is it that your job isn't quite paying enough?
Is it that you want more time for holidays, more money for luxury items?
Is it that you want to be your own boss?
Is the business you have generating loads of sales but not a lot of profit for you to make use of?

I have been involved with hundreds of businesses, from million pound a week turnover to only a few thousand- margins vary from very little on each transaction to quite chunky- in the end after costs they all roll out with a profit conversion that can be reinvested in the business, marketing and deliver either for investors (Plc, business angels, one man bands the whole lot) or the owner operator.

I also have been involved with businesses where liberating the cash out of the business has been really difficult, loads of businesses that the measure of success is suppressed by the lack of cash flow.

First meetings with these businesses are about the following, or themes around;

1   Giving the key people the time back to work on the business, not in it. (Don't chop the carrots in the kitchen when you can be marketing to people to come and eat them)

2   Implement marketing that is measurable, cost effective and you can turn on like a tap (Manageable, Measurable and Repeatable)

3   Sort out the cash flow- you want the business to have spare to do with what you want, not to just suck up to keep itself running

4   Create systems that answer questions for you without the need to be the font of all knowledge- get the time back to **work on the business**, not in the business.

Be an Action Jackson!

1   The biggest difference in success is keeping going and gaining momentum- once it starts to roll then keep it up

2   Set yourself the time to take the action- Operation Time Commando (link below) has loads of tips to help with this, the key is making sure that you set yourself priorities and objectives that you know you can achieve. Calendar blocking is a great start for uninterrupted time.

3   Stretch yourself because often once set up you use the tools and methods again and again but without the need to put in the leg work of the set up.

Boiling Down to the Brass Tacks

The list here are the key areas to cover for developing a Cash Flow Fountain that you can systemise and develop for the long term;

1   Build an Asset
2   Grow Lean
3   Be in a market that is already working
4   Be different in the marketplace
5   Measure your marketing- Return on Investment
6   Eliminate, Automate and Delegate
7   Reinvest to Grow
8   Systemise Marketing
9   Roadmap the Business

This is where we start to put your plan together.

Build an Asset Not an Income

The biggest difference between the day job crowd and someone who has to be concerned with cash flow is that you are not trading time for money.

Whether you are hourly paid or on a salary you trade time for money- this is why many employees feel that they are making somebody else wealthy. Often true.

When you have your own business you do not trade time for money in the same way, this plan will show how you can ensure that the money you receive is no longer directly attributable to the hours you put in, this applies whatever the business is you operate.

Over time working with your business to generate cash flow and build an asset you are winning twice over- the business itself has a value over and above the cash you have drawn out of it for your own lifestyle requirements.

The employee sees their salary increase over time- let's say its 10% increase per year. They have the income from a job role doing this- if they put 10% of this salary away each year they have a little savings to spend. They have not got away from the income and expense cycle.

Where a business owner puts 10% of this "salary" back into the business it builds the asset value and this has a spinning effect of building the value of the business that could be sold on- this is how the owner becomes wealthy when they want to sell the business. The business owner is spending money building their asset.

This may be spent as marketing money or growing the operation so that you do not just buy yourself a job through operating the business.

Watch out that you do not continue to work in the business and not on it your Cash Flow Fountain is not going to excite you. Think of a driving instructor with one car- this guy has bought himself a job, if not driving then he is not earning.

Have a school with 10 instructors who pay a fee to him for filling the book or take a salary that is less than the hours for lesson price earnt and the top man has the cash flow. He can also take time off when he wants, in addition he has the time to work on the business (marketing, networking and recruiting more people to be his instructors) He is no longer sitting with pupils exchanging his time for money.

As an another example here is an extract from advice to one of my clients;

"Work ON the business not IN the business. What do I mean by this?

If you could send 50 thank you cards and 50 birthday cards on a Monday afternoon rather than taking 2 hours to pour drinks, this activity will cost you let's say £15 in team wages covering you on the bar.

The 50 thank you cards have a 10% response because you put in a small bounce-back offer, and generate sales of £25 each. That's £125 income.

The birthday cards however have the same 10% response but the average sales are £45 (bigger party). £225 in sales.

So far your two hours has brought in £350 worth of sales, Depending on your conversion rate this could be profit of £105, less the 2 hours, let's call it £90 extra profit for 2 hours work.

Do this for 3 "occasions" in the week and that's £270 x 52 = £14k"

This example shows how the measurable and repeatable activity can help drive cash flow through the business.

You will have equivalent promotions available to you- birthday contacts are a really straight forward one to start with and are a manageable promotion to send out, and handle the influx of increased customers.

Cash Flow Fountain Taps

Across so many business and a long period of time I have found that there are common threads to help you get a grip on the journey to cash flow mastery. A lot of these will be familiar to you, it is how you put them together and catch yourself doing the right things more often.

What Do You Want?

If you want to start a business to be rich then fair enough, it's a goal. If you want to replace your day job salary with your own business income from cash flow then this is also a great goal and target.

If you have your eye on a new luxury watch in 3 months, or you want a second hand sports car in 6 months, whatever it might be you need to know how much this is and have specific targets.

The specifics are what are going to help you build the plan and make decisions for your business as you progress.

Writing down your targets are going to make the difference, what is your net profit goal for the future? Using your goals you can calculate your annual net profit amount, this is useful as it also allows you to put a value on the business you are building, this asset value is important as it does two things.

1   Reminds you that you are building an asset not just "buying yourself a job"

2   Has your business value in mind- depending on your sector there will be a common multiplier for someone to put on the business if they want to buy it.

For example a contract cleaning firm I know of is valued at 3 times multiple of it's value- however the owner has personal net income, and grows the business, of over £100k. This is a large value because he has a great cash flow coming off this business.

A public house though has a lower multiple, because although the cash flow is there, the flexibility and nimbleness of this business is lower, the liquidity is really low for someone who might want to purchase it. There is good cash flow and profit, however you are really limited in where you can go, other than more of the same.

However a good pub with food should still have a value of £250 000 at this lower multiple.

At the other end of the scale "Apps" for mobile phones and the companies that make them have massive multiples- the reason? Write the product and deliver it to market once, deliver millions of the product for limited cost, with limited "people" cost to service this, unlike the cleaners or waiters in the other two examples.

So what do you want?

Write your requirements here;

Monthly Net Income	
Annual Net Income	
Asset Value Multiplier	

Now you have it here, write this on your white board, your notice board, a post it for your dash board, (again it sounds a bit hokey but it is a reminder for you to take action and keep the momentum going) if this is something you really want you will make sure that you do something every day to get you towards the goal.

If you have a photo of the expensive watch, luxury car, holiday destination whatever it might be to keep you focused close to this then so be it, either way the cash flow and income is what will make you be able to achieve these goals and enjoy the profits and motivation benefits of excellent cash flow.

Mapping the System

Over my career I have been on both ends of plans and activities, whether this is a marketing plan, sales plan or a system for the operation that is tried and tested to deliver a consistent outcome, a sales script, dish specs or marketing plan.

All of these methods are a means to an end, they make things a little more predictable, enable you to measure how things are going, did it have the same or better result as last time you did it?.

I am a big sports fan and like to see how the coaches of different sports make the small differences to achieve their goals.

In cycling the Team Sky mantra of "marginal gains" all the systems and methods, equipment, analysis, nutrition, rest patterns, own pillow to sleep on, warm up and warm down....the list goes on, all of these items have an effect, they are worked into the "system" in the Sky team particularly to get a result that is better than the rest. It is repeatable because there is a Roadmap to deliver on this.

The large branded operations, even with multiple brands under one company have a way of doing things they, (and me personally) have trained and coached general managers from multiple brands in the same room, the same Roadmap to success.

This was to show that the building blocks to success come from the same place and that each step has to be taken in order.

Building Your Success Path

We have taken action already to build the business, today we are going to start to draw up the Success Path, this is how you will build a profitable, cash flow positive business to ensure that you stay on track, Action Jackson's know that this is vital.

You will gain clarity on why you are building the business, know what to focus on in your business and what you can have other people work on for you.

You will reduce the time taken finding your way, you will also be prompted to involve others to develop your Cash Flow Fountain.

Building the Success Path ensures you get to your destination faster, speaking with many business owners as cash flow comes up they either tell me they would love more or assure me absolutely that this is the key to a successful business, it is the lifeblood for both your motivation and also to allow you to follow the path that you want to take.

The Cash flow also allows you to focus on only the opportunities that you want to follow rather than being tied up in working in the business instead of on it. Working *on it* is the key to moving to the next level.

Taking steps to build your system and ensure there is a Success Path for others to follow as you move on to operating the business in a new way. You will have more freedom this way and also be able to start new ventures.

This Success Path will assume that you already have the business running, even though it may still be very new. The benefit of having this available is that your team can refer to it and you can measure against it as time progresses. There may be a need to return to the beginning of the Success Path processes to either put things right or indoctrinate new team members in the "why we do things like this round here" method of induction and development.

Success Path activities will be highlighted as you progress through your Cash Flow Fountain Plan.

Lean Mean Fighting Machine

The way to start a business with very little money is to be super lean- keep your costs down, it might seem like a good idea to have a little office with a nice desk and new computer to set you off on the right foot.

At this point it is likely however that you are the only employee of the business, why add an overhead now that needs to be paid for out of your cash flow- this cash flow is at this point, in priority order funding marketing, creating cash flow for stock and new products or just being money you wanted to spend towards your other personal goals. The office is not required, and is not a lean machine option.

Investing in complex equipment is actually spending on bigger overheads that you cannot avoid and cannot escape from- they really only give you a large bill and reduce your positive cash flow.

Looking for innovative ways to keep your positive cash flow and have money for the marketing, stock and things you want should be a priority.

This will be covered later, I just want you to **check your behaviours** right now and question yourself as to whether the nice office and new computer are really keeping you moving towards your goal or is it a nice to have that **erodes** cash flow.

The other item to consider at the outset is your margin, keep costs low and profit margins high.

I have worked with restaurants and bars over many years, often the easiest advice is to put up the prices.

In an ideal world be **the most expensive** place in town with the biggest margin, there will always be a market for the cheaper product or lower margin, there will also always be a place for the top end in the market too, this is your part of the market.

Sometimes you need to add perceived value to the product or service you have, sometimes it is just having the confidence to ask for the price. If you are in a service business practice asking for your big ticket price in front of the mirror, worth checking how convincing you are and also that you can keep a straight face ;)   Think 25 Euros for a burger in a European Ski Resort for example!

Reality is, for the best chance your margin needs to be as high as you can take it, this is the cash available to you- I will cover price setting later- however a good starting point is to check what the market charges and make sure you are at least 20% more than that! You need to have the confidence that you are the best and you will be in demand.

Practice asking for the price, even when you have no other work on the books stick to it- make yourself slightly unobtainable, you are in demand after all. Always ring back rather than take a call straight away. I generally shy away from contractors that can fit me in straight away....why are they not busy?

You don't have to worry about risking a lot of money to get started in your business, these principles are setting you up to ensure a lean mean business that produces cash quickly and more effectively than you previously have.

Things to check off to keep you lean;

1 Can you run the business from home to start with?
2 Do you know anyone that can give you basic accounting advice?
3 Do you know anyone that can give you some basic legal advice where needed?
4 Do you know someone who you can trust to bounce ideas off and act as a coach?
5 Do you need to set up a company structure? Quite often you don't

6 Have you run any of the following types of advertising before;

A Search Engine Optimization
B Twitter boosted ads
C Facebook advertising and Facebook paid for boosts
D You tube Advertising
C Postcard Advertising
E Direct Mail and Lumpy Mail
G Lead pages
H Newspaper and trade press adverts (could lead to a lead page/squeeze page)
I Pintrest programme
J Advertorial newspaper articles

7 Do you know any companies that are likely to use your services or business now?

8 Do you already have customer or prospect databases that you can utilise?

Taking the Leap Of Faith

Many people who will be reading this will have a small business now and want to see it become more successful. With better management of the cash so you can get out of it what you intended.

Alternatively you are currently employed in a normal job and want to move forwards and have a future under your own control. Removing the security of a monthly salary or weekly pay, but also giving you back the control that is limited by having your future in someone else's hands.

I have worked for others and myself over the years, (I do well in both environments) I think that when you are an employee who knows that you can make money from other streams and your own business you become a lot more relaxed in the paid for job, you know you won't be floundering if you lose it!

The great thing about the regular job alongside setting up a positive cash flow business is that you have a monthly injection of cash each month where it's required, you are your own investor as well as getting the business to a positive cash flow position quickly, if you can continue to put some of your seed money in for the first 6 months as well as reinvest your profits for growth the speed that you move your business on will be great.

You CAN do it, I wrote this book alongside a large operations management role, grew profits in my day job on a year by year basis, researched and set up the online element of Kings Of Cashflow AND I have 3 young daughters with their own interests that need the car-pool, class time, costume and make up commitments sorting out! I am not super-human... you can do it with a little discipline. Just a couple of hours a day, 5 days a week will do it, be honest you can miss the TV Soaps, can't you?

You are working on putting your future in your own hands, in addition you will not find yourself out of a job looking for a role with others with similar skills.

Looking around the country when you see the changes in for example coal mining- the last coal mine closed at the end of 2015 in the UK- all these highly paid men with specific skills are looking for jobs in an industry that no longer exists in the UK, they all finished on the same day, live in the same area and require a job...not a great position to be in.

The same with power generation as the old technology is turned off and we switch to other methods, the people working in the coal fired stations will all finish on the same day, with the same specialist skills, living in the same area.

What happens if the London company decides that it no longer wants a Cardiff based call centre but wants it in Leeds or in another country....same again.

Having a business with strong positive cash flow insulates you from these uncertainties, ensures that you are adding value to your area, builds a good income for you and your family and puts you in charge of your own destiny.

To be successful you will have to take some risks- with the plans you create from the points in this book you will have to take some calculated risks, minimise the areas that jeopardise you having positive cash flow. You can build the business in your free time, the reward is worth it in the end.

Take the time you spend watching TV or catching up on social media, the time that you are able to invest may only be a couple of hours each day, but soon builds up.

You may have to tweak your original plans, you will have some uncertainty that you have to handle, the graph that you will see of your progress will not have a straight upward line. There will be some plateaus and some downward points- keep pushing on and you will get to the goal you are after.

When you check in on what it is you trying to do and the reasons you want to do it they will be compelling, jot some of those down here, I'm looking for the top three reasons why? They could be financial freedom from being an employee, having extra cash for luxuries, ensuring you can help your children achieve their goals or their short term consumer needs (a car or help with study fees perhaps), they will be compelling but also personal.

Jot them down and in the same way as you have before with target earnings write them down where you can see them. This is your commitment to your future;

1 Family	
2 Financial	
3 Freedom to..	

You also need to address the fear that is creeping up in your mind, be positive!

You ARE ready to build a successful, exciting, cash flow positive business! You ARE willing to do what you need to be successful, take the educated risks and do something each day to move you towards your goal! You ARE ready to do this today!

What Business Are You Going to Build?

Look at your skills, work through the things you use each day, how can you make them better, what do you do online that you could make better, think about the things you like to do- what can you do to make your hobby or interest easier, better or provide information on?

Jot down as many as you can- how can one of these things assist with another interest- do you see an application you use at work that could be used in your hobby? Do you know an importer that you can help them with their route to market, do you have a network that you can provide a service to that you have a different angle on that then becomes your product or service?

I know of people who make a good income, part time from their interests, whether this is a guy selling £10k a month of golf equipment from his garage through an ebay shop or a young lad selling remote controlled car parts through ebay and making £2k a month (he is 13).

Another friend of mine used to bring in high end watches and sell on a website he built with GoDaddy.com.

People who love what they are doing, do a little research and set themselves up with good cash flow businesses- from home, part time and apart from the wrapping (they can outsource) limited work on their part.

Set up on Amazon and you can have this "fulfilled by Amazon" a small payment to them to essentially wrap it and send it out for you- all you have to do is get the container delivered directly to their warehouse, 24 hour availability and they process your order immediately not when you can get into the post office or have it collected by one of the parcel firms from your home.

Work through up to 20 of these ideas, even the crazy ones will have a nugget in there for you, we will narrow down the field a bit later, for the moment brain storm your interests, skills, work knowledge and improvements for things you use now.

Loom bands which were a global phenomenon were a forgotten item that someone made with their grandmother years earlier, they remembered the time they enjoyed, created the loom to make it accessible to all and BOOM a massive multi million pound (fad maybe) business with massive cash flow and a global appeal.

<u>1</u>	
<u>2</u>	
<u>3</u>	
<u>4</u>	
<u>5</u>	
<u>6</u>	
<u>7</u>	
<u>8</u>	
<u>9</u>	
<u>10</u>	
<u>11</u>	
<u>12</u>	
<u>13</u>	
<u>14</u>	
<u>15</u>	
<u>16</u>	
<u>17</u>	
<u>18</u>	
<u>19</u>	
<u>20</u>	

Business Models

Other things to think of;

White label products- find a supplier, create your own brand and sell through routes to market that are already set up, therefore eliminating a lot of your overheads.

Ebay and Amazon can assist with this for ideas. (Alibaba is where to start for suppliers).

If this seems a big first step follow through on the same activity with products that are already selling, you can sell them under licence from a wholesaler.

Just get something out there so that you can learn how to do it quickly. The more mistakes you make with a low level of risk the better, just take action.

You will practice headline writing, photographing the product, starting a buzz about the product, picking out the hot sellers.

Mobile phone apps- you can have apps built on your behalf, you are a consumer what can you do to move this on.

Information products- you are reading one, and I have more than 10 products (some of which show you how to do the same) that I generate a list for and sell on a month by month basis, in addition I have a monthly recurring paid for newsletter.

This is a model that you can follow, find your niche and realise that your skills, hobbies and insight when produced logically for others to consume can satisfy a need, and is high margin.

All of these are potential start-ups and/or something you can run alongside what you are already doing, they are things that can be "add ons" and can move you forward quickly. There is a lot to be said for starting now.

My information products would assist you in driving these businesses forward, my mission is to enable you to be the best you can be, they will pay for themselves when you implement the information in them to your business.

As a Cash Flow aware business owner, using the knowledge you have here you will ensure that you stay focused on making sure it delivers for you, and you implement the Corner Stones for success.

To transform your lifestyle and obtain free cash flow tools, implementation action sheets and access to your £200 market critique visit KingsOfCashflow.com

Email: Stuart@KingsOfCashflow.com

PART TWO

TURN ON THE TAPS

Getting Your Customers. This Makes the Money!

When I boil down the bulk of my business this is the item that makes the biggest difference and is also the area that many business owners miss the trick with.

If you make the best radiators in Europe with the most energy efficient way of working in a changing market place as we become ever more aware of the environment that is brilliant. I would imagine that you have the features pinned down, the benefits for the customer and a few industry plaudits too.

Also consider this before you start- Apple are not selling phones, their real business is ITunes, you have to go back for all your apps, music and updates, and you pay every time. Load up the tune once, millions pay. Where are you really making your money and are you marketing this properly? Cash flow and a constant supply of new product that they don't even make themselves. What is your real "end-game" to make the money?

Before you start work on the best water boilers with all of the same sort of credentials what is the business you are in?

You are now in the "Marketing Radiators" business- you need to find the customers, tell them about the product and get them sold, if you have the calculations right your cash flow will be positive and you will make a profit from positive cash flow to keep moving the new business forward, the business of "Marketing Radiators".

Same applies if you have a restaurant- you have the best décor in your field, the most highly trained team serving the customers, the best product to make the best steak. Anyone in the restaurant yet?

If they are and you have done no marketing this was word of mouth, the cheapest form of marketing but the hardest to get. Social media and other review sites will help this spread, and of course you can boost these.

However in both these businesses you want reliable customer flow that you can build over time, continue to contact and ensure that you have measurable return on the activity that you undertake. Every business works well with a database and direct marketing by the way.

Marketing is not complicated but you are looking for the method that you can ensure there is a Return on Investment and it does what you want it to do over time.

Your Marketing Needs to Be Managed

The marketing needs to be managed, this is more than putting money aside for advertising. What you have to remember is that the people who are selling you the advertising space are getting a bonus on selling the space. Their need to have your advertisement work or drive customers to your business is nil, their job is to sell you the space.

To build the cash flow in your business then you need to build the customers in your business, your responsibility in the business is to put customers in front of your product or service, as time goes by and the business gets much larger you may have others help you with this and manage certain parts of the marketing mix for you (social media presence for example).

At this point you need to handle this yourself, giving you the great opportunity to pick up on customer needs as well as show your product or service to them.

Your Marketing Needs to be Measured.

This is the only way that you will know what your Return on Investment is- with this information you will know what routes to your customers are the best ones, you will also then know which of your marketing methods to crank up your investment in.

Don't rely on one or two methods but understand which messages have the most impact with your customers- generally telling them how you can solve their problem/need is a good starting point rather than how wonderful your product or service is.

Your Marketing Needs to be Repeatable

When you know that your marketing is being effectively managed and you can measure the returns on it <u>and</u> ensure that it pays off you can then pump money into this.

You will find that its impact is multiplied, the more you put in the more comes out, this is how you can build the business quickly and if you have set up at the outset with a business that can have strong cash flow you start to make the money through your economies of scale.

The more this is automated you will find that you do not have to take on more people to deliver to your customers and you can manage the business effectively, the last thing you want to do is overwhelm your fledgling business with a number of customers that it cannot handle.

Watch yourself here....you probably love having great ideas, you probably love the set up side of things, the excitement of new logos, new products, setting up your network, thinking of who you need to be in touch with to get everything just so.....does this sound like you?

As covered before you are now in the Marketing business, the business that brings in the customers to use your product or service, in turn this gives you the feedback so that you can go again and continue to market this product or service.

Hold off starting the next one, hold off adding a new line to your business, get this bit right, this is where you make the money that builds the cash flow that enables you to keep moving forwards.

What to Charge?

Hopefully by now you know that you don't want to be the cheapest in the market, how do you beat the guys who have the lowest price?

Sometimes the low price can put people off, for example knowing where to get the cheapest diamond ring may not really help if your wife wants the added cache of going to Tiffany & Co. Same diamond + added value (that little blue box)

The steak served in your local restaurant is probably better than that in the chain steak house, if you don't sell on the personal touch and the ambiance then the customer knows the steak is pretty much the same and will choose the place that gets the economy of scale. (You lost on price and reliability to deliver).

My youngest daughter was watching Masterchef and could not believe that the celebrity chef in her words was "charging £100 for the same bacon as she could get from the butchers".

I gave her the insight, restaurants are not about the food, they are selling an experience. At this she told me she loves Pizza Hut, I do too but I don't go primarily for the food although I do like the Deep Pan.

I told her I'm paying to watch her enjoying herself, the self-serve salad, drinks and ice cream. Pizza Hut know it's the children that decide where families eat when they dine out.

You need to review the business with these things in mind, many of the extras that you can add to the business proposition can cost you nothing (you were doing it anyway but you accentuate the positive).

Would you rather buy a living room suite with a 10 year guarantee or without?

Giant offer a lifetime guarantee on their bike frames, the guy in my local bike shop assures me I will be sick of the bike and want a new one before there is much danger of anything going wrong with it. But I would buy the Giant because of the assurance rather than risk my investment.

They probably sell more bikes and in comparison to the number of times the guarantee is used it is worth doing it for the lifetime rather than the 5 years of the competitor brand, (the cost is zero) if there is a problem with it you will find it in 5 years I would imagine….

You could offer an online video link for a diet plan to go with maybe a pedometer, or a chin up bar comes with a link to a video that shows lots of different adaptations to make the most from your physical product.

After you have made the video the link is effectively for free after a few sales, this added benefit enables you to charge more for your product or service, increasing the cash margin and the cash flow.

The market is going to set your price not you. Check the market and how much similar are being sold for, add on the extras, others will have them, work out what they are adding on for the extras this is your edge to keep boosting your cash flow.

Inexpensive ways to add value to your proposition in the market place.

The market will want to come to you even if you cost them a little more.

Avoid having the Rolls Royce product in a market that only wants to buy a Ford, you won't sell at the cash flow level that you want- added value is not added complication or cost to you and the customer.

Building A Brand

Sorry to break this one to you- you don't have the money to build a brand. Gucci is a brand, Adidas is a brand, Omega Watches etc....

These companies are working with image for their marketing and an association with the brand and what it stands for.

I've been lucky enough to have 4 Mercedes cars now, nice car. I have never test driven one before I have placed the order! Why would I....it's a Mercedes...

At the level we are operating we are not building a brand. Yes a good reputation a name for a product or service that people recognise, even if you have a logo and identify this as your brand I'm happy to roll with that, but you are not in the same position as the above.

Your marketing efforts need to focus on the **Manageable, Measured** and **Repeatable** approach.

Knowing what to do more of to get the best return from your money is vital, with that said though there are really cost effective options that you can take to advance the business and the cash flow you are looking for these include the following;

A   Word of Mouth
B   Pinterest
C   Twitter feed marketing- accurate and targeted based on likes
D   Instagram- this is to build a following that then can be used to steer towards your product
E   Google Adwords
F   Search Engine Optimisation (can be expensive and varies)
G   Facebook boosting- controlled cost and is as accurate as having a database of ideal customers
H   Postcard marketing (see my own postcard marketing guide)
I   Asking for Referrals through networking
J   You tube vlogging
K   Wordpress which is a blog that you can then insert videos and links
L   Database marketing/Customer Relationship Marketing

When using social media it is worth remembering that if you fill a "timeline" with your business people switch off and block you, if you are using a mix of social to build a following then you should consider the following recipe;

Social post, social post, interest post, sell post.

At this level you can build your "tone of voice" and a rapport with potential customers, but they still know what you are doing.

A couple of good firms to look at for the difference between a brand and a business building a following are;

Tag Heuer aspirational with no sell. The characters or simply global sports stars and movie icons. The association is with the high performing stars in different fields. Buy this product and a bit of their glitter rubs off.

Oipolloi of Cottonopolis is a clothes shop in Manchester and now London. They have a shop dog for interaction, who doesn't like to know what a cute dog is doing? You meet the "characters" who model/work in the shop, they direct you to a product to buy on Instagram probably every 4 posts. They are selling a lifestyle/fashion that you can belong to.

The Rock the wrestler turned actor is one of the most influential users of social media for selling product and controlling image, you could argue he is a brand of his own.

Michelle Lewin is a "fitness model" and posts aspirational photos of herself, workouts you can repeat and occasionally products to buy, her mix is less sell more buy into being like her, she is self promoting to remain key in the industry she works in.

Implementers Box

In this implementers box work at reducing the list down to the ones that appeal to you or you have seen your market competitors using to good effect;

Marketing Method: Instagram	Yes or No
Do I have knowledge of how to access this method?	Yes, my phone
Do I know someone who can help me?	
Can I do this cost effectively?	
Do I know how to measure the effectiveness without it becoming a job in and of itself?	
Will this reach a large number of the people I know will use my product or service?	
Are my features or benefits easily communicated through this method?	

Once you have these answers what are you going to do next? What action needs to happen to make a difference to your cash flow?

These questions should get you a good start on which to target as your marketing methods, the easiest may not always be the best but if you can answer the later questions positively then easy or hard you can quickly learn the skills and implement.

The implementation is what will make the difference to the cash flow, not the great ideas.

Measuring the Impact of Your Marketing

You need to know the profit that is associated with your marketing not just the top line that is driven to the business. (Top line vanity, bottom line sanity)

It is quite straight forward you need to know how much you spend on the Marketing method and the campaign itself. Hard cash- this is cash flowing out of the business, it needs to bring some back in with it for positive cash flow.

Next you need to know how much in Top Line you have brought in and then the Gross Profit, this is the profit that some call the operating profit. The money that comes in less the cost of sales, nothing else. The labour bill, electric bill and so on comes out of this operating profit.

You now know by taking the cost of the campaign away from the Gross Profit, if it was effective or not. At this point a positive number will do the trick.

If it is positive then there are only a few things to look at, how many people followed through on the marketing, how many people actually bought something. Sounds obvious but if you don't get many people interacting with you then change the pitch of your advert or lead page, or who you are targeting.

If loads interact but nobody buys then you need to check out how easy you can make it for your customers to buy with you. Have you made it really obvious?

Utilising Contacts

I use list brokers to help boost my database of customers, I also pay for clicks through people with great lists. Now this is simple transactional stuff but effectively they have a rich list that I want to have access to, I can build the list myself, hope to target the same people or just tap straight into theirs by paying for it.

I can control how much I spend by putting a limit on the spend and only agreeing to pay for a certain number that sign up to my list, over time the cost of the acquisition goes down as they will eventually buy from me (some drop off, but that's the way it goes).

The way I market means that the 5% who buy there and then a lower priced product cover the cost of the total acquisition of contacts. I don't need any more than that because ultimately I want the contact to market to on my own list.

Now look at it another way, you will have contacts that have customers that you would like to build a relationship with over time. How much are you prepared to give them for the sales contact?

If you sell a product for £50 with a cash margin of £30 are you prepared to give them £15 of that for you to grow your business quickly by having access to their customers?

Equally if you are prepared in your own business to pay £50 to acquire a new customer for the list give the person who is now your affiliate the whole £50- the profit at this point is not your end game.

This is common for some businesses particularly where a company is looking for new products and services and sees that for them to develop it and move it on quickly is more effort than utilising you as their contact.

They don't have the cost of development, customer service and so on, your economies of scale are exactly what they don't want to add in!

The Big Goal

The Big Goal is probably that you don't want to feel as though you have just bought yourself a job with your own cash flow.

There will be a time when you are the only employee of the business you are setting up, the benefit is you get to learn all about the business in all areas and you can make all the decisions (whether you want to or not)

The Big Goal is to be able to work only ON your business rather than consistently IN the business doing as Stephen Covey says in 7 Habits of Highly Effective People the "thick of thin things".

This is the restaurant owner moving from chopping the vegetables to marketing the business and managing it, to employing a day to day manager and being able to oversee a small number of venues, probably with a small team of operational and marketing managers looking after the day to day.

This is very possible by the way, I know personally 3 people who are millionaires through expanding their businesses along this path. When they can work ON instead of IN the business the BIG gains happen.

Set yourself a goal of when you will be able to work ON the business rather than solely IN the business.

You need to weigh up at what point can you let go of some things, even if you don't employ someone full time you will be able to outsource people who can do specialist roles or even some of the heavy lifting of the day to day tasks.

Implementer Box

Target Date for the BIG Goal	
Target Earnings the Business Needs to Let me Do This	

Now you have these details you can work backwards from the price you are charging and the number of customers required.

You will not be able to leave everything behind, but you will be able to get to a point where the day to day is overseen, and the big picture is what you deal with.

Systems Always Win!

On your journey to the BIG GOAL to work only ON the business rather than IN the business you must find ways of getting things done without the Thick of Thin Things getting on top of you.

You are building a Lean and Mean Cash Generating business you need to be aware at all times of adding in costs.

At some point they will be necessary, this might be an upgrade to a computer, a system that helps you to automate customer contacts, or even taking on some team members to do the routine activity that ensures you have the time to carry on with the items that move the business forwards.

You can find yourself if you are not careful sucking up the profit and cash through spending it on things that don't make the difference to the actual profitability.

Systems always win…cash flow and time management.

The easiest way to look at this is can you **remove** the problem that sucks up your time and money, can you **automate** the solution?

Building the business you have been keeping things lean, as you built it up you will have been working hard to keep the cash in your hand instead of pass it out.

By automating customer service best that you can, or a query line leads to a FAQ sheet that someone can access you are automating the solutions- giving you the time to work ON the business, saving your cash flow and ensuring you do the work once but get it to pay off many times.

After all of this you will get to a position where you can delegate.

Looking at a public house or restaurant for example, you may end up having an onsite manager then you have 5 venues with 5 onsite managers, and then an area manager that looks after the 5 while you work on new opportunities.

All this is possible but comes at a cost- by this point the cost is paid for by the cash flow and you are the hand on the tiller that keeps things going in the direction you wanted, **NOT** the hand that pulls the pints on a Friday. I'm sure you can see where I am coming from.

If you have an operating system and a manual on how to do everything you can get to this point, (additionally you could sell your system to others), that has great cash flow!

It also adds value if you sell. In service businesses you can utilise outsourced home based employees from ultimately around the globe. Using Elance, Odesk, linkedin, Craigslist and your own contacts- these people can either be flexible to suit your needs and budget or in the case of some of these people they are much cheaper than a "home" country based worker, but you are still paying well for the work they are doing in their home economy.

This is a more common method than you may realise, the English abroad is good and can be great for maintaining your cash flow in the business.

It's fair to say that most businesses when they start up don't always put in place the infrastructure and systems that a larger organisation would have. It's just generally you, your idea and a business plan.

But setting up good systems early on will save you money, hassle and frustration in the long run and you certainly can't grow without them.

Here's an example of what I mean; imagine your business is delivering barrels of beer. All you need is a mobile phone and a truck to get started. You can get by with an order book and an invoice book. Now imagine that you have grown to 20 trucks with 35 drivers doing 135 deliveries a day.

For starters you will be sending out about 2700 invoices a month; if you could get 50% of the invoices automatically generated and sent by email you'd be saving yourself 1350 stamps not to mention the printing and envelopes as well as the admin time… You may even get paid a bit sooner which helps your cash flow.

Your simple business just got complicated by scale. And systems are needed, put good systems in place early on and processes so that when the business multiplies you are not pushed under.

So here's a little list of things to consider:

Infrastructure - are all your PCs, servers, laptops, devices, networks, security and backup systems all up to the job?

Email and calendars - a good email system will share calendars and act as an archive. With the right set up it can then be linked to a database for reliable, cost effective and measurable marketing.

Financial systems – apart from the tax and legal implications, a good financial system provides regular indicators of what's working in your business and what is not.

Customer Relationship Marketing system - these can be general or industry specific. At the start this will probably be a list or an excel spreadsheet, but should graduate to some kind of system. (Aweber and Infusionsoft for example)

This is absolutely invaluable in terms of keeping track of interactions with people and other organisations. Key to sales growth and part of your marketing strategy.

Document management - be organised from the start. Work out a system with backup which you can keep adding to as you grow. And make sure everyone who needs to, has access to it.

How Much Do You Need?

Getting it Going!

Typically this is what you will need to consider for starting up, **your goal is to have great cash flow**, the less you keep putting in the better.

Essentially the list will run to at least these;

A   Cost to talk to the accountants and solicitors
B   Set up the company
C   Create the product or service
D   Website
E   Marketing seed money
F   Product development
G   Postal costs
H   Database ongoing costs
I   Stock/product to sell

Consider your sources of money to get things going- for example your family members may have some money they are prepared to invest in you and your business to get things rolling.

You will probably have local "business angels" who for a short period of time (couple of years) will lend you money to get things going with a fairly easy way out on repayment, they don't want a piece of your business they want to see you get it going and then with their repayment covered they move on to the next one.

You could use a bank of course but they will charge interest and are no further on from the Venture Capitalist who will be putting pressure on the business and you to perform so they get their return.

There is your own funds if you are setting up next to a day job.

You also have the possibility to have partnerships where you perhaps take on the lease of a pub or restaurant and pay a rent but everything inside the building is yours, including the ideas on the menu and the way you market them, this gives you access to what you want to do without the need to risk large amounts of capital.

Last but super risky because if it goes wrong its really expensive, credit cards…a friend of mine now has 25 late night bars- started with his business partner from 2 credit cards they maxed out….lucky and they knew what they were doing as they essentially do for themselves what they previously did for others. A massive risk but good luck to them….I would rather not take that amount of risk….be calculated with what you do (for them it was a good calculated risk and they soon paid them off from the cash flow in the business)

Momentum Building

There is a Snowball effect that you want to achieve with your business and cash flow.

The BIG GOAL of working on your business will come from this Snowball effect. We want to trigger this so that you no longer go from one month doing a great marketing job and then selling to all these customers and then the next month having to do the same thing all over again.

To get out of this cycle, (which is no more than just having given yourself a job), working in the business to generate sales you need to reinvest some of your money into the business, this might be for a multitude of reasons; which one and how much for you?

Implementer Box

Reason	How much profit %
Marketing	
New products	
Strategic network building	
Customer relationship	
Branding of website	
Outsourced team members	

Depending on your business you will have other lifeblood things for the cash flow to be reinvested into to grow the business and get to the BIG GOAL covered earlier in this book.

For resources to forecast your cash flow and check your plan and progress visit KingsOfCashflow.com

PART THREE

MAKING THE DECISIONS

Making the Right Start

You should now have a list of business ideas- from this we are going to select the right business for you to be in. You can also assess whether you are in the right business now if you already have a service or product that is already set up and operating.

For great cash flow it might sound obvious but you need to buy or produce a product or service at a lower level than you can sell it at.

On top of that is the cost of marketing the product, this can be done really cost effectively and with a clear measure of Return on Investment.

You also need to know that where you find a market that others are making a lot of money from, this is not a barrier to you being in that same market. You know that people are already interested in what they have to offer and that you too can sell to that market. There is plenty of space in the market for you, and as the new starter you will not be noticed by the big players for a long enough time that you can get established.

A good example of this is looking at the coffee industry in the UK, in 2000 there were hardly any coffee shops as we know them now...Café Nero was a handful of shops in central London, Costa was nowhere and even Starbucks had a very low representation across the country.

So Nero set up one street away from the high street because they know people will go a few hundred yards out of their way for the cool brand that they are, but no more than that. Costa and Starbucks choose sites positioned where loads of people pass, they are where the money is.

Over recent years there are loads of "Artisan" and local coffee shops some have other things connected, maybe a farm shop, bike shop or art gallery. This is their point of difference that gives the customers a reason to visit, over and above the cup of coffee.

This is how they can go where the money is and compete with the big brands. They also use to their advantage the marketing ploy of local business supplying local people, a ploy that costs nothing.

Inventing things can also be expensive, you may have the great idea or product but are you a great marketer?

The skill that pays the bills is sales and marketing, inventiveness is important but the money is the priority to keep the business alive.

Cash flow for the business and yourself will be what keeps you going and is the reason that you got into doing something for yourself in the first place.

What Identifies a Cash Flow Positive Business?

The positive cash flow is the easy answer, but you don't want to find out by just giving it a go and finding that there is not any cash there.

There are Key Identifiers for spotting a Cash Flow Positive Business that you can employ before you sink money into it.

At some point you have to take the leap of faith, but you can do this in a risk savvy way rather than just taking a chance. If that was our method we could go to the Casino with a strategy and hope for the best (by the way the casino company built the building using positive cash flow)

Just covered the first 1, but to spell it out...

Number 1- Go where the Money Is

You need there to be lots of people who want to buy your product or service, there are massive markets that you can be in, when you are out and about and you spot the plumbers and electricians vans, think of the last time you tried to have a tradesman come to a quick job or a painter be available. Tough to remember when any of those guys were easy to pin down?

So they are in a market with loads of potential customers, they have their service to sell, they have their overheads....there are more than one in the area that you live but they all seem to be busy?

You now know where I am coming from, the Market is plenty big enough to stand multiple operators....when you are next near a cinema count how many restaurants and fast food places there are.

They know there are lots of people there who will buy, they know that they are in a big market (food and leisure) but people will choose their preference, not on price or sometimes even service just their preference. All of the places will be busy.

When looking at your business ideas, find the market, see if it has plenty of operators in it and how they are doing. If all looks good don't be put off and get in there, as you can see from the examples above there is enough money in the market to keep everyone busy and making a good living.

At this point I would steer clear of really big ticket items with highly specialised markets, there may be good margin in selling for example precision oil cutting equipment or specialist computer parts, but how many customers do you have available to you, maybe a handful of major players globally, they already have more than enough suppliers for this currently.

Even if you are the best at this is there enough money in the market and enough customers for good cash flow?

A strong cash flow business is information products-you have at least one if you are reading this, depending on the business you are in you will have access to products I have written that go from less than £20 all the way up to £300 for one set of action guides. The business is built on the lower priced products in less of a niche. (The highest priced manuals are for pubs and restaurants, they cover operations as well as marketing and ROI)

The cash flow from the Pub and Restaurant system is a little less than the other products, the list of potential buyers took longer to grow and is limited to those that are happy to take at least some advice or tips and apply it to the business. A lot of pub operators do ok and are not always happy to take and implement things that someone else who is not serving the pints and food to their customers is suggesting.

Fair enough- my cash flow comes from general business that applies many of the same marketing principles and activities to their business. They get the results and we are all happy.

Number 2- Is there longer term large profit potential?

To check on this requires a little bit of market research. In the market that you want to be in have a look at the range of prices for the product or service that you wish to be dealing with.

A couple of examples- if you want to operate a pub or restaurant and sell a sirloin steak there is a fairly narrow range of wholesale price for the steak in the big scheme of things.

However when you look at the retail selling prices there is a much broader range. This will be calculated not so much from the wholesale price that they buy it in for but more from their business model.

Things like, the margin they want to have after all costs are paid for, the number of chefs and waiting team they are happy to run with and the rates they are happy to pay for them. The other costs of the business tied up in the fixtures and fittings, costs of marketing and so on.

For me as mentioned before keep the margin for yourself high, there will always be a market for the premium operator and if set at the right level there are enough mass market customers who want to also get into this part of the market.

A good example is also around the premium that Apple can charge for the iphone, I'm not a whizz kid on knowing all the intricacies and ultimately pay your money and take your choice, however the iphone can charge a premium based on its desirability in the market place, as a phone from the reviews lots of phones do a better job. My own iphone, if it rings, takes email and lets me keep track of business it works for me, camera, music playback speakers, game play…not so much, still got one though!

Number 3- Economies of scale

Most service based businesses have the problem that the more customers that you add to the business you generally have to add an overhead- that overhead is the team members you have to take on to service them.

If it is a restaurant you need more waiting staff- one more for every 4 to 6 tables is common, so if you start on a Friday night serving a restaurant that has 12 tables full at a time then that is 2 chefs, 3 waiting staff and someone to run the front of house, double that and you are looking at 6 waiting staff, probably 2 people to run the front of house and another chef.

The economies of scale don't really help- the raw ingredients (the food) just keep contributing at the same level per guest, the only thing you really are helped by is the electric bill and maybe your rent if you already had the capacity in the room- they won't really change.

Similar for service companies where you visit customers with your skills, to service more customers with your expertise you need someone else back in an office to process the mundane/ routine part of the job, this adds cost including the building, extra computer for them, benefits and so on.

You have more business but the economies of scale are missing and your profitability is missing- you have the same cash margin per customer (sometimes it may drop).

Businesses that would have greatest appeal to having great cash flow are where the size of the operation does not have to grow significantly to service more customers- this is where for example information products work well, or perhaps mobile phone apps (you can source people at a reasonable cost to do this for you).

Amazon/Ebay businesses are also great in that you can have someone else facilitate the delivery for you, the cost is paid for by the customer. The more products you have delivered makes no difference to your time but your cash flow increases on the Economy of Scale.

You do the work once and the end user does not require your overheads to be building to service them. It may be that you need a virtual assistant or to have an auto-pilot enquiry system working for you as the business scales up but this cost is not going to move in a linear way with the number of customers you have (unlike say a painter and decorators).

Number 4- Small Start Up Costs

There is no need to have loads of money to either start your business, or if you have one, begin to turnaround its fortunes with small investments in the right areas that you get a good Return on Investment.

Pumping loads of money into a new business at the outset is fraught with danger- you don't know if there are some lessons to learn as you build up.

Build up, don't splash your hard earned money, use the initial cash flow of the business to pay for the growth, if like me you start alongside a normal job then you have a budget each month for your expenditure based on your salary.

Think of the business as your home budget. You can't keep spending if you don't have the money there…but when you see it come in you can use a little in the right places.

Anything more than a couple of thousand pounds should be re-considered (even if the business as an idea is sound), some of your costings for a business that currently has no customers, no presence in the market and no positive cash flow of its own requires thought. It may only be a tweak in your route to market or the way you are going to advertise, look for where you can get the cash flow going.

Number 5- Longevity

Assess the business and work out if it has longevity- we don't have a crystal ball for all of the changes that happen in business and the way that markets change but with all the information that you have available to you now weigh up if the business has got the legs to last the next 5 years.

On the internet lots of people get stung by the changes in rules on say Google, or with "Search Engine Optimisation", they may be building what they think is a great business by knowing the loop holes and how to make money. When the internet companies either change their rules or decide that they can monetise the service the business model either changes dramatically for cash flow or dies altogether.

I know really successful online business people who went into meltdown for months as they needed to change the way they built their lists or find that they had relied totally on a loophole that was no longer there.

A mistake I see my clients making before working with me is often they don't look at their marketing for the long term. They find they have to essentially build the business every month for the bills they have to pay. The marketing does not build a relationship with the customer that they can use again and again for one another's benefit. They don't make good use of database building, (it's often just a list of names) and lost the value of maintaining contact with them in the long term.

Assess your business ideas from earlier against these parameters

Implementer Box	
Go where the money is	
Economies of scale	
Is there long term future	
Small start-up costs	
Longevity	

The Excellence Equation

I attended a great seminar around Personal Excellence, and this boiled down the recipe for personal excellence to an equation, this equation can be used to review other things too, it also provides a good guide as to getting your house in order to move your business idea on from a page that says it should work to a position that you can make it earn you money.

The Equation is this;

Excellence = Believe x Attention x Technique
        in Potential

*The seminar "Personal Excellence" written and delivered by Nicholas Bate

Belief	Attention	Technique
Belief drives behaviour, behaviour drives results	Nothing happens without attention	Find the best technique
Beliefs are both empowering and limiting	Love the plateau, this is your virtuoso moment	Learn it from a practitioner
There is no failure only feedback	As time moves forward your competence improves	Apply the technique, check your implementation and make it your belief
You can do anything, but you can't do everything		

You can apply this to yourself and also to your business, do you focus on one business at a time or try and run a couple of ideas and see which one takes off.

My view is that your day job if you still have one is now well within your scope and you should give it your full attention when that is what you should be doing. However when you can give yourself clear time to get your business going then follow the Excellence Equation.

You need to believe in the business potential, not a dream, work through the exercises again from your notes that are there for you to implement and check that you are sound in your thoughts.

Give it your full attention at the times that it is your priority, a couple of hours a night with no distractions is plenty to move things along quickly, the same couple of hours you probably used to watch TV....

Technique- this book is to give you techniques to find a business that has strong cash flow, the techniques that you can study and use to make those assessments.

As you will see at the back of this book there are range of products that will give you the technique to move an online or real "bricks and mortar" business forwards and make them either profitable from the outset or a greater Return on Investment than you currently achieve, all of which are measurable.

You may not see immediately that it applies to you and your business, but nearly all of the techniques have got the scope to be used in any business. Just believe in the potential, give it your attention and use the techniques provided.

This is where I save you the time so you can spend that time building a strong performing, cash flow positive business.

Cash Flow and the Excellence Equation

Looking at the two options- Build one business or five at once- let's say that you have the same amount of time in the week to complete the work as the person who chooses to do 5 at the same time.

You give full attention to the job at hand, applying the techniques to the business to really make it progress to positive cash flow, you forecasted that this would happen at 8 weeks.

Everything goes to plan and sure enough you are in positive cash flow.

The rival who starts 5 business at the same time only has the same amount of time to focus on the job at hand, this is split across the 5. Keeping the cash flow masterplan in mind they do not take on any other team members to help move it on.

Now they are also successful and their 5 business come through with positive cash flow as they stuck to the forecasts- however it took until week 40 for this to happen.

The thing to have in mind though is that you have built the knowledge from driving the cash flow in your business in the space of 8 weeks, it is likely you had a couple of problems that you learnt from, also likely you had a breakthrough moment that you jotted down and now know makes a big difference, you start a second business in week 10.

This takes you 5 weeks not 8 to get to positive cash flow....business 3 takes 3 weeks....if you are set on having multiple streams then you can get there with more pace, you are also now the "practitioner" in the Excellence Equation. Your rival has to wait 40 weeks to get there.

The Excellence Equation does something else for you, makes you execute your ideas as a business person. At some point someone has to do the "doing" part of the business, there are loads of business ideas raining down on the earth every day. The difference between inventing the multi-million selling super mop and it being a great idea is just down to someone getting out there, getting it made and getting it to the market.

I made the same mistakes- spending time on the perfect product package, spending loads of time on a logo- in the end you need to execute and implement to see the benefit of starting the business and the cash flow that comes from it. That is one of the reasons I have the implementer boxes in this guide.

As a long term client working with me you will always have an implementation plan that you can apply to make sure you carry through and make it happen, not move on to the next great idea. I agree some of these implementer tips are the same, they repeat, some of them seem like back to basics, in the end they will help you get things done.

Choosing the Option to Pursue

So far you have a list of potential business that you have an interest in, after that you have looked at the 5 key areas to filter this down to business that will stack up for good cash flow quickly.

Finally you have the Excellence Equation for both you and your interest in the business and how you can move it forwards, and as a secondary filter for the business itself.

I can't make the decision for you in this area, however the crunch time is here. Be aware that you will not carry things off perfectly at each stage, you are also likely to have some problems along the way- all that considered though none of this will happen unless you take positive steps now.

You will learn faster actually getting on with it than watching from the side lines, you can't learn the game unless you play it, whatever that may be.

Creating a Championship Winning Support Team- Accounts and Legal

Start now…your cash flow is king and you want to protect this without introducing overheads into the business.

Top tip though- at some point you will need an accountant, maybe also a business solicitor to keep things moving smoothly and stop you being distracted from driving the business and results forward.

Research them now, jot down in the implementer box below the names of two accountants and two business solicitors.

You don't need to contact them or have them on the books but you will need them at some point.

Other good things to research are printers for potential marketing materials and maybe a virtual assistant to take customer service calls as and when required (especially if you have a regular job in the day and cannot do this yourself, and you should not if you are paid a salary).

Implementer Box

Accountant 1	Address	Telephone
Accountant 2	Address	Telephone
Solicitor	Address	Telephone
Printer	Address	Telephone
Virtual Assistant	Address	Telephone
Business Coach	Address	Telephone

Don't get too tied up in the set-up of the company just yet, if you are not in a regulated business that requires you to be registered as a practitioner in that field you can retrospectively set things up. In the short term you will have to keep track of the income and outgoings of the business yourself in a simple ledger or spreadsheet, but as this is the whole point of driving cash flow this should not be any extra work.

Any small business accountant will be used to dealing with this, in the UK you can even start a business in one tax year and not have to submit any documents until the end of the next if you so desire-accountants are used to covering this off, they just don't like it because they are the type of person who likes order and things to be in the right place from the outset, it is not out of the ordinary.

Choosing a company name at this point can be as simple as using your own name, as a sole trader even if there is someone else in the same field, doing the same thing as a sole trader, if you do not just rip them off you can trade using your name, after all it is an accident of birth and naming.

As time moves on if you want to set up a limited company or similar then you need to have the name checked out and also look into the legal requirements of having directors and that the company name is not someone else's trade name. It matters more than being a sole trader and you should check it out.

Building the Business

You have now selected the business that you are going to work on, you want to be super focused on what you are going to do- you need to know the main features and benefits of the product or service that you are offering.

This sounds like salesman training, but ultimately that is what we are now moving into- you have the product or service identified- the market does not know about it, the features and benefits are what will make the difference to it having an impact. Jot down what these are in the implementation box;

Implementers Box

Product or Service Features	Product or Service Benefits
1 40% alcohol gin	1 Appeals to gin aficionados
2 Lifetime guarantee bike frame	2 Peace of mind on big purchase
3	3
4	4
5	5
6	6
7	7
8	8
9	9
10	10

Self Funding v Getting Funded

Don't be discouraged from getting started by thinking that you need lots of money to get going- now there is no doubt you need some money to get going. You need to produce a cash producing business when you start with your own money. Your own money will potentially run out quickly if it is not producing a positive business cash flow.

My own business was started with limited cash. The initial cash flow over 6 months was from my own pocket with cash flow supplementing this to grow faster. I gave myself a budget that I was happy to put at risk, but started with a plan to ensure that my marketing plan was self funding. I also limited the speed of the growth in this way but my risk and exposure was measured.

The benefit of running your business via the "Self Funding" route is that you learn how to control the costs as well as invest wisely to keep it going. You can learn to be an efficient business and become efficient at having positive cash flow.

The alternative is to find funding from someone else, (whoever this may be), they are likely to have a share of your business, and because of this they also have some control.

At this early stage for the benefits detailed above I would recommend the self-funding route- you can learn other lessons on running an efficient business at the same time as growing that business.

You have total control on the direction it goes, the money you invest and probably make better decisions as it is your money that you are playing the game with.

The opportunity to take funding from someone else may well likely be available further down the line if you wish to expand quicker than your cash injection would allow.

There is the price to pay, but once established you are in a better position to potentially pay this investor back and get them out of the business quickly, giving you back control in full of the expanded enterprise.

Making Your Mark

You want to stand out from the crowd even though you know this is where the money is- how do you do this?

Could be that your service or product has more features or benefits than any other? Could be that your ongoing service and customer support is more than the competitors? Your reviews could be the best. The personal touch that you offer.

Don't get drawn into it being about price, as covered previously there is always a market for the premium end of the market, the lowest margin needs the most sales to enjoy the cash flow fountain. Your enjoyment of your business will come from the extra cash flow from making your mark in the market place through these differentials. I know for example that I am an implementor, I am not the visionary ideas man- but visionaries more often than not need someone like me to make things happen. This is my niche, there is only 1 implementor for every 4 visionaries in the business world, I am a commodity.

Be clear now on what those differentials are. For my own business I seek to enable others to be the best they can be, my goal is to move customers from a "one time" purchase through to being a multi-product buyer, then ultimately that leads to the ongoing monthly client, via the Inner Circle newsletter and recommendations for the best Return on Investment for their business.

Now this is also part of the business model- this business guide leads to a relationship that over time leads to ongoing clients. These ongoing clients will be relationships that I know drive Return on Investment and profitability in business. What I get out of it is enabling others to be the best they can be and for me a great cash flow business.

So look at what you are doing, what are the top things that enable *you* to make your mark?

Riches in Niches

Over the years I have heard this phrase more than once, the Americans pronounce it "nit-ches", in the end all it is getting at is that when you focus on a specialist area, service or skill, product or answer to a problem then there is enough money to enable you to have a good business.

A friend of mine works only with Dentists, enabling them to market their business well. He knows that a dentist may have lots of skills, but they are probably focused on the treatments rather than the marketing of the business. His business provides the service that gets this working for them.

His own lifestyle is the one he has created for himself, he is able to live in Spain, has hobbies that he has time for and is able to work with his wife and has plenty of time for his twins.

Look at your business idea, whose needs does it satisfy? Are you focusing on the one small question that they need answering? You will be more able to do this than answer everything and maintain your cash flow progress.

Through my whole career whether working for J D Wetherspoon, Café Nero or passing my finance and stockbrokers exams, the key motivation was always to help others reach their goals and enable them to be the best they could possibly be. Nothing else…

My own business is -as above- all about driving Return on Investment for my clients, the products may do this in many different ways but they all lead to the same place, things you can apply and measure cost effectively for a Return On Investment, on line or real physical businesses. In short implementation.

Behind this is my real reason for being, helping others to attain their goals, my broad knowledge and the skill from a wide variety of experience ensures that I can help others and deliver transformational results.

Just do one thing really really well for the Niche that you identify with and from your previous activity you know is going to give you a positive cash flow business that you can develop for the next 5 years.

For your gateway access to the range of products and a FREE assessment of a current piece of your marketing plan, worth £200, join me at the page KingsOfCashflow.com

Email: Stuart@KingsOfCashflow.com

Building Your Championship Winning Support Team- Outsource

You have the idea nailed down, you want to implement but there are a few obstacles still. You don't have all the expertise in all the areas to do what you ultimately want to achieve. There are ways around this that are cost effective, highly professional and enable you to be innovative as well as quick to the market.

You are building some **momentum** now behind your plan and you should be getting **excited**.

Great resources to help you move things along are Elance.com, Odesk.com and upwork.com, these sites put you in touch with freelancers all around the world who will work up ideas, reports, product designs (99designs.com is also great for this, loads of designs but only pay the winner), apps, research, web sites, online marketing, logos the list goes on. This book cover was designed by someone on Fiverr.com

The professionals who are on these sites are paid either by the hour or to a fixed rate that you agree with them at the outset of the job. Go to the site enter what type of job you want doing and fill in the job form…select from there.

This enables you to get things done, sometimes alongside your day job, without it being your time creating each line of the product, the speed and momentum in getting product or service to market is what keeps the cash flow going in the right direction for you and the business itself.

At this point take time to work out what you need to get your product or service created- the sites above will help you do this.

If you want to build a business that you create a product or brand and sell this on either through your own website, ebay store or "Fulfillment by Amazon" you will need to find a supplier.

There are multiple places you can go for this however if you are looking to have high volume finding manufacturers abroad helps with the cost price and they are also flexible and wish to do business with UK and other customers in the global economy.

One of the best sites for this is Alibaba.com, they literally allow you to search for the product that you see is the niche you want to be in, you contact the supplier through Alibaba.com (they also vet the companies) and start your negotiations.

This route may seem scary but you can scale up to this with your own brand- creating a business for the long term (over 5 years) that you can sell on if you want as it has its own intrinsic value beyond just the products.

How Do You Know If You Need the Help?

I run a really lean business, applying the cash flow principles that are identified here, you need to evaluate depending on your business who you may need to help you with your success. I use Aweber for automatic list building, Paypal for payments and subscriptions. Book covers are outsourced, so is website building and hosting. I utilise a printer that can post out my newsletters as part of their service, so I don't have to, cfhdocmail.com.

Use the tools and systems that keep you focused on what you do well and eliminate the time suck that comes with trying to do it all yourself.

Keeping your team accountable so that what you want to happen does, at the pace you want to is absolutely key.

So for example if you are dealing with the designers that are through Elance you really need to be thinking of ensuring that your instruction is clear and concise, explain in your instructions exactly what you want- the time taken now saves the message going backwards and forwards that costs time, or equally something that is not to the remit you thought of but did not communicate.

Both of these are frustrating and eat into your time and ultimately your cash flow for the business.

There are benefits to be had from doing things on line, chief among them is keeping down your overheads and being able to communicate quickly.

On the other end of that though if you are in multiple time zones in different parts of the world you will have to consider this for the service that you can offer or your network is able to deliver for you.

Nothing here is a problem it just needs to be considered.Use the Implementer box below to cover this ground;

Supplier and what they do	Positives	Pitfalls	Select y/n

PART FOUR

STICK TO THE SUCCESS PATH

Success Path: Why You Need One

You know when you set out on a trip around a city that you don't know you either use your Google Maps or the local guide from the travel centre.

The Success Path is what you rely on to get to your destination. It is tried and tested and the route it will suggest makes sure you get there with best efficiency, even if that takes in the sights for the best experience.

To make sure your Business Cash Flow Fountain stays on track, these Success Path Insights can be taken in isolation or together to make sure that you continue to have the impact that you are looking for on a day to day, and a week to week basis.

Success Path: You Are A Marketer

If you ask people to tell you about themselves at a party they normally tell you what they do, rather than about themselves. Many people are defined by the role that they have at work rather than looking to what it is they really do, their job title rather than the added value they give.

An Operations Manager looking after a large team is "helping develop people to their full potential", and should introduce themselves as such. A financial advisor "enables people to reach their long term financial goals", these are much more striking than just the job title.

Regardless of the job you have, the business you run or the product type you have, to get the most out of your Cash flow Fountain you must appreciate that you are now in the Marketing of your Business arena.

The customers that you service, (in whatever field you are in) provide the cash flow that you can now use for the identified needs you personally have.

To improve your long term financial position this distinction between job title and understanding your responsibility as a marketer is key. Without marketing and a system to attract and retain customers you will be hoping that customers come to you, and return. Having them return enables you to reduce your cost of acquisition, increase the number of products you sell and drive Cash Flow further for profit.

Cash flow and Marketing go hand in hand, as you build a solid cash flow plan, alongside are simple action points to build reliable, proven marketing methods to make your business bombproof!

I was working with a sizable leisure group that had this issue. The team at the front line were squeezing the cash flow by not fully understanding the business that they were in.

Speaking with one of the very knowledgeable bar managers he had the idea of making his branch in the business famous for having the best and widest range of rum in the city.

This guy was an absolute expert and knew from conversations that he had with his close customers that they had an interest in the idea.

He proceeded to order in the rum range, great products to be fair to his knowledge- many I had to be educated on even having worked in the industry for 30 years and built spirits ranges for hundreds of premises over time. All the way through to products that cost £200 a bottle to buy in.

The retail price was £7 a shot, cost price £6.60. He could not ask anymore as he was already way beyond the price anyone would pay for a shot. No cash flow here....

To add insult to injury the small operations team overseeing the multiple venues did not know about this stocking policy and were not marketing it either. All in all this was a total of £1400 worth of stock on the back bar and no marketing to get rid of it. The whole team had forgotten about telling current or new customers about this new range and how it would enhance their visit to the bar and introduce the customer to something they had never had before.

The turnaround came from a two pronged attack, (they had not been my client for long) part one was building a story up around the products, not an education more a "can you believe that rum costs this much".

The local paper picked up on the incredible price per bottle and did a lot of the advertising for the venue effectively for free through the stories. This was quickly followed with a window poster and A frame to encourage people to have the most expensive rum in town.

Marketing came to the rescue of the cash flow problem.

On the back of this I encouraged them to sign people up to a mailing list for the long term marketing benefits. The rum sold out, the venue had a list of 137 new customers to market to and people knew that this place was somewhere to go to find the "out of the ordinary".

In this way the venue had driven people in to buy today, they also now knew that these people lived close enough that they would visit, that they were interested in the rum (maybe just for the curiosity, but they were interested all the same).

The venue also had the knowledge that these people would respond to marketing that drove them to take action.

The data that the venue gathered asked for postal address, email and date of birth. The date of birth was under the guise of this being a drinks promotion that you had to be aged over eighteen to participate.

The venue now had 137 customers that they could contact directly, 137 people who they could invite in for a Birthday event, probably attending with others. 137 people who they could invite in with for Valentine's Day. 137 people who could come in for Christmas parties....the list goes on.

By having the postal address there would be a higher "open" rate than just having emails that can be just sent to a spam email address and never see the light of day.

This business had control over its cash flow from this predictable group of customer relationships.

This can be followed up with other lead capture activity. Bounceback vouchers given out in November and December in a bar that invites people back in January and early February. Using a package that gives the customer confidence that they will get a square deal at a set price at this time of year is really powerful.

The bounceback to be "cashed in" needs the contact information to be filled in, easily done at this quieter time of year as the guests are enjoying their meal.

They go back into your Customer Relationship System. In this case though they are meal package customers. Sending them a meal invitation for the month of their birthday is likely to be taken up. This is evenly spaced business all year around and the principle can be adopted across any business type.

Success Path- Explode Your Profits

There is a large gap between the business that is ham-strung by the ability to pump up the cash flow to a point that the owner can move from the day to day business to being an entrepreneur who can expand quickly, have other investment opportunities that they are able to take advantage of, and the alternative where you have freedom with the decisions you can make for the business and your own financial future.

The business that is ham-strung with a direct line of improvement of perhaps 5% to 10% growth each year lacks strong cash flow, they are adding a new product line, hiring another member of the team or 2 or able to increase their price marginally in an incremental way.

This is only moving the top line a little- the Cash Flow is not improving per transaction, the business has just got a bit larger. The work to convert to profit stays the same and probably suppliers have squeezed up their prices too.

The goal with the use of Cash Flow Fountain and reliable marketing funnels is to enable you to make the right choices in the business paths to follow- adding another string to the bow that grows profits by explosive levels, the kind of profits that convert to the bottom line to enable you to buy the choices that you want for your business and personal freedom.

A business owner I have known for almost 20 years and who has a copy of my Pub Marketing System has other businesses, which have come from the cash flow from the original set up.

The cash flow from his public house enabled him to use the outbuildings of the premises for an "Outside Bars" business.

This business provides the drinks at major events from vans and lorries that have been kitted out with full bar equipment and pumps. The beer is supplied on a sale or return basis for stock thanks to the top rated events that are his target market. The supplier could not get the association with these high profile events themselves!

In addition the trucks that house the bars tend to pay for themselves after their first few events. The cash flow that they produce is huge, fueling further growth and his growing property empire.

This is a great example of cash flow enabling an Entrepreneur rather than just a business owner.

Success Path: Advertising or Marketing?

Return on Investment (ROI) is key for ensuring that your Cash Flow Fountain continues to flow strongly.

This needs to be something you build into your marketing as measurability. The response rate you get against the cost of the marketing shows you the return on investment and the cost of acquiring the customer.

A good shift in your mind for the long term benefit of the business is to think that you are marketing and selling the first product to "buy" the customer and their contact information for the long term.

When you have this you can market directly to them with less inducement to trade with you. This in turn reduces the cost of acquisition and makes your marketing activity predictable **and** repeatable.

Advertising should not be confused with Marketing-advertising is about image and one off sales, the people getting rich are those that are selling the space to you in the newspaper, radio, online or on poster sites.

First step is to formulate an offer with the sole purpose of gathering the direct contact data of the new customer- this is lead advertising and is very different to basic image advertising- the goal is the data not the sale.

There are two main types of offer that encourage people to give you their contact details for the long term. These are either information orientated or built around the product and offer itself.

Some examples of information orientated offers include reports, brochures, online videos, downloaded MP3's and buyers guides.

Those that are product and offer orientated include discounts and vouchers which you could call "paper offers", they are only a piece of paper but they are cheap to produce and easy to administer.

Packaging of products or perhaps the value of future discounts, service or entry to a loyalty scheme all of these demand the customer contact information to access them.

The best example of this would be the Tesco Loyalty Card. In its prime this card enabled Tesco to learn the buying patterns of their customers, predict what they would want to buy if they knew Tesco stocked it, offer deals on these products and all the time the earn and burn rate on the points was unrivalled in the market place.

The card and everything that went with it was a perfect Customer Relationship tool, and helped fuel the growth of Tesco.

The beginning of the end of this place in the market could be pinned down to when the company halved the value of the points that they awarded.

They may have reduced the cost to the business but they also switched people off to using the card and also the company itself.

Tesco without this data also found it hard to re-engage with the customers, leading to the problems in the early to mid 2010's

As a smaller business you can use a multitude of less complex systems than the Tesco Loyalty Card used. This requires you to utilise what are perceived as old style and expensive methods as well as online methods.

Direct Mail and postcard marketing coupled with a follow up and voucher scheme lock your customers into you for the long term. These methods allow you to be specific with the message that goes to the customer, be direct in the offer that they should have and build relationships for cash flow and profitablity.

These principles can also be applied to email marketing and online activities- the return rate is highest for physical rather than digital campaigns, but the same principles apply.

Build a list, then add detail for this to become a Database, use this on a consistent basis to keep yourself in your customers mind and make you the first choice for them. You will be able to add simple details such as the business type, buying pattern, most purchased item and so on over time. All of these will enable you to build offers and promotions that will satisfy what will no doubt become a group of customers with similar needs that you can satisfy as a business.

Systems such as Infusion Soft and Aweber will enable you to combine online and offline communications and offers, cost effectively and time efficiently to continue to secure your strong Cash Flow performance.

In addition to using these systems there are good printers that as part of their business will fulfil your direct mail pieces from your database.

Although at first glance they look expensive, printed documents ROI is high, they demand action with the correct offer and copywriting. They can be tracked and they are predictable. Many of the other methods have a lower level of penetration with the customer that do not drive action, reducing your cash flow and undermining your ultimate goals.

For your gateway access to all of this and a FREE assessment of a current piece of your marketing plan, worth £200, join me at KingsOfCashflow.com

Email: Stuart@KingsOfCashflow.com

Success Path- Use A Rifle, Not a Blunderbuss

Knowing how your ideal market is made up, and the problem that you can solve for them is vital for your Cash Flow Fountain and the Marketing that drives the pump.

To protect your cash flow the approach to your marketing needs to have an outlook that ensures when you fire the shot it hits people who will want to become your customers for the long term. Identifying who these people are for most businesses is the key to securing long term profits

Reducing the amount of general advertising you do to find customers is a key step to strong cash flow. When you know that your marketing activity goes to customers you have a relationship with, and the needs that you can satisfy your profitability per customer increases.

In addition you know that your campaigns will have a measurable ROI. Through direct marketing methods the ROI will be strong and predictable- both assisting your cash flow and ultimately company value.

When loading the rifle instead of the blunderbuss you need to be accurate about identifying the "who" in the marketing- how you can satisfy their needs, match the desires they have and answer the questions they have.

If you know the "who" then you will have the confidence that the activity you are conducting will enhance and not detract from the Cash Flow Fountain. You are boosting the pump station with qualified customers relationships rather than vague advertising.

These same principles apply for online businesses as much as they do for "real" bricks and mortar premises that have been established for many years.

Success Path: Turn the Pump to Full On

Depending on your business there will be lots of methods of getting yourself in front of potential long term customers. How many are you using though?

If you were to list how many you are using I would imagine that you will find that either you have only considered or are only using a few. Things move quickly in business. One thing to have in mind though is that your marketing messages will stand up to every outlet of communication that you can think of.

I recall speaking with a colleague of mine, and the conversation went something like this;

Richard- "I've invited the social media guy along to present at the meeting today, I must admit I don't really see all the benefits"

Me- "You remember how you used to do mail shots, flyers with promotions and adverts in the magazines?"

Richard- "Yes"

Me- "Well just think of social media as the same as all those methods you used to do, it is a bit of Emperors' New Clothes, but the principles you used then stand up today"

Richard- "As simple as that....."

Me- "More or less, you still need to drive an action from the customer, the drawback with social media is that you struggle to track the returns unless you incorporate a voucher or show me the phone angle, but you can build that in. Impressions and views don't help you want to know who has done something about the offer"

Richard- "I thought as much, pretty simple then"

Me- "Yes, just about...." *both laugh

The point here is that all of the different outlets for your marketing ultimately are a different means of carrying your message. The goal for these is to either induce someone to give you're their contact details through a lead obtaining piece of advertising, or to communicate the offer to the database you have built up of switched on eager and regular customers.

If you can think of 3 different routes for your message- keep building that list to at least double that and push your message through all of those- this will explode your profits to a new level, and your competition will wonder how you are able to keep spending on acquiring customers.

The more complex your array of outlets for your marketing message, the wider your range of methods the harder it is to copy and compete.

Large organisations in whatever business you are in will not be willing or able to do what you are conducting as a fully aligned, complex system.

Success Path: Why You?

Reviewing the fact that you need to be where the money is, the obvious question for your potential customers is "why you?"

Why should people do business with you rather than a competitor, what is your unique selling point that puts you ahead of the other businesses that are in your sector.

Identifying how you can solve the problems of your customers to the best effect can get you on the route to understanding what this difference is.

You can be in a busy market place with lots of competition and use this difference in your marketing.

Are you faster at doing what you do, can you add value that others cannot easily do, is your guarantee stronger than others.

How can you work on these to make them even more of a reason that the market chooses you?

Once you have acquired them as a customer you can leverage this further through your ongoing communication and relationship building activity that will drive the business for the long term through a strong Cash Flow Fountain.

Success Path: Systems Always Win

A large part of my career I have been a "multi-unit manager" for large companies, typically covering a large geography with complex businesses and large teams in each. I have been responsible for up to 36 businesses at once and over 1500 team members.

The only way to do this effectively is to use systems.

These systems in part are set up by the type of business you are in, the legal set up that surrounds the product can dictate part of how or why you have to do things.

If you are service based company you will have systems around delivering the service, if you are a manufacturer then the systems will be to deliver the product with minimal defects. Your business may be somewhere in-between these two extremes.

Either way to extract maximum cash flow and profit from the business a system will enable you to manage things accurately and identify and correct problems quickly.

To get the most from your Cash Flow Fountain you should develop systems for each area of your business. Getting the product sold should be the goal of one of the first systems that you build.

You want to have the confidence that you can attract customers, extract contact information and other data, and continuously follow up with them in the long term. A database (rather than just a list of contact names) enables you to have the insurance policy of regular customers that you know. Regular customers that you know you can contact profitably and boost cash flow at will.

Direct marketing methods with good copywriting and follow up will ensure that your Cash Flow Fountain flows freely.

Make the right decisions in choosing the business that will have this cash generation for you and your family and your long term business success will be much more secure than one where you have to advertise again and again each month for customers that are entirely new to you and your business, only to be lost again next month to start all over again.

Introduce a low level paid for email newsletter with a voucher included for a greater value than the price of the newsletter.

Use the money that comes in from this as your marketing budget- it is predictable and will continue to grow your Business Cash Flow Fountain for the long term and transformational results.

Additionally the customers will come and buy your product, you build a relationship with them (birthdays etc) and you are paid multiple times for writing the one newsletter.

Success Path: Insulation

I qualified as a Stockbroker and Financial Advisor, after the crash had occurred. This was a good time to be building a business in this field, ultimately a sales business, and a great experience in answering customers' needs.

One of the reasons it was a great time to be involved was some of the lessons I learnt and could apply to business later. It also gave me insight into investments and financial instruments that help in my understanding of general economics and business.

During this time as general FTSE 100 share prices' had dropped significantly it was an ideal time to buy shares in companies that were not that risky. Why? If you had already bought shares at £1.50 each and the price went down to 50p, when they increase in value to the market rate you would have in effect bought them all at a discount against the market valuation. The shares you held at £1.50 have been diluted by the others and you are insulated against future volatility.

The shares you could purchase when others may have been exiting the market have insulated you against the vagaries of the market for the long term.

Systems, direct marketing and strong cash flow are the insulation against the volatility in whatever market you are operating.

Through implementing the plans in this book and taking massive action you will ensure your business is both profitable and predictable.

As you acquire more customers and more importantly their contact details, and an understanding of their needs and wants you can answer their needs more readily for both yours and the customers' benefit.

Success Path: Principles Run True

Regardless of whether I have worked with major high street brands, small chains, loose groups or absolutely bespoke offerings in the service or product being offered to the market, the fact stands that through most businesses the same Principles Run True.

Being able to take on the approach, marketing, operations knowledge of others that you are either the customer of or meet in your network groups always look to adapt and adopt the Principles to both Cash Flow and Marketing and transfer into your business.

Too often I hear about how businesses are unique, so different to others in the same marketplace that they can either survive by not getting involved in the market or equally when they need to work hard to survive they continue to use the same old (often ineffective) routes in advertising for one of visits or transactions from customers. The work on building a relationship of any description has not been done.

Protecting Cash Flow by knowing the Return on Investment (ROI) of your different products and the marketing campaigns that go with them is vital.

This book continually reinforces that a Cash Flow Fountain built from choosing the right path in product, sales method and market position will be successful.

A strong, measurable and predictable performance from your marketing activity comes from developing leads from advertising that then builds your Customer Relationship Marketing Activity after that.

When you click into noticing this in your own work you will notice more and more how companies induce you to give them your contact information.

Standing out from the crowd after that is then the challenge when you have this information.

Couple of quick examples I noticed on the day of writing this- the "NOW" series of music compilations has a competition to win a wireless speaker. Aimed at a teenage market this probably has appeal, they have an email address and smart phone, perhaps requiring a wireless speaker. Just send the email and phone number to enter the draw....

I use a cycling brand called Rapha, nice kit but a definite premium offer- they sponsor Team Sky. The big Belgian Races are underway, through social media there is a contest to win a bundle of kit by predicting the time that the winner will complete the race distance. Just send in your email and phone number to enter the draw.....

In both these cases the people who are entering are "pre-qualified" through their interests and the fact that they are interested in the prizes on offer.

Adaptable to your business in one way or another and not rocket science?

Success Path: Implement! Implement! Implement!

Setting yourself up to succeed is one thing, actually getting around to it is another thing altogether.

This book is set out deliberately to give you time to take in the information and then do something with it- a day to take it in and set yourself up for what you will be doing next.

You may not hit all of the deadlines at the pace that I have laid up for you, however implementation is what will make things happen not reading about it, working up a plan and wondering what it will be like if either it goes well or goes badly.

Implementation is key to seeing how things work in reality in your business. Direct marketing and a customer relationship marketing programme will add predictability to your performance and growth, still needs implementing though!

Through having implementation at the forefront of the tools you are going to use, (create a system in your business to help with this, including using outside agencies to do the grunt work for you), you will ensure that you avoid the disaster of "I'll get around to it".

With multiple levers to pull in your customer marketing strategy and using the 10, not 3, outlets that your competitors are using you will be implementing more and faster than the rest of the market this is how you will ensure that the massive action that you are taking turns into truly transformational implementation.

Where To Next?

Dive in- you have the resources and basis of your plan from the Implementer boxes. Transfer these to one place and use these to hold yourself to account as you get started with a positive cash flow business.

As added value to the book you can access various resources through KingsOfCashflow.com including a cash flow forecast Excel sheet so that you can play around with the numbers and see how your business can grow quickly and cost effectively.

There are also links directly to some outside agencies that can ensure that you don't do all the work yourself, and move quickly from ideas to action and implementation then further to sustainable profitability.

As for what I can do for **YOU** now acquire your free cash flow forecast tool, progress and comparison charts and submit for review a piece of your marketing for an assessment worth £200 join me at the www.KingsOfCashflow.com

Conclusion

I know that if you have a little bit of money and a good idea you will achieve your goals, creating and owning your own CASH FLOW FOUNTAIN will give you the financial security you want- above all you must take ACTION!

Epilogue

You've made it to the end of the book, and I would imagine you have a new found confidence and the framework to get your Cash Flow Fountain flowing with the taps turned full on!

Maybe you are filled with hope that the choices you can make with strong cash flow will make themselves available to you, dreaming of the extra profits that you can choose to spend on your priorities, moving from trading your time for money and replacing that with a predictable income that you control....

Next thing to do is to actually DO SOMETHING! Procrastination will defeat you if you don't carve out a couple of hours each day to make something happen.

Block out a couple of hours each day that is dedicated to your Cash Flow Fountain, once you get going you will find it easier to "have time" to get things moving.

In just about every business I know when you get the momentum going in your direction it has its own snowball effect- this snowball effect is what leads to you getting a lot done, and then this leads to massive results

So next steps- take your ideas, work them through the system and turn on the taps to YOUR OWN Cash flow Fountain

I'm confident that through implementation you will be successful, don't hang on to things if they are not working, go through the steps again with an improved or enhanced offer, your first option is unlikely to be a home run!

To your success

Stuart Bowker

PS: If you find that you want more proven systems that will give you predictable returns on investment and are measurable and repeatable head to CapitalThomas.com/transform for your gateway access to further insight and an assessment of a current piece of your marketing plan, worth £200, join me at www.KingsOfCashflow.com

Email: Stuart@KingsOfCashflow.com

About The Author

Stuart Bowker has a broad experience of fast moving businesses, across hospitality, retail management, and personal finance. Stuart has studied and implemented direct marketing methods for over 20 years.

He has a unique ability to identify systems, add value and insight to them and make them work for others. These systems and methods have been used for his own businesses and the benefit of others to extract greater profit from new and mature businesses.

Stuart lives in Yorkshire with his wife, 3 daughters and 2 dogs, a keen cyclist he still believes he will break through as an International Playboy in the style of Mario Cipollini the Italian sprint cyclist from the 1990's.

HERE'S WHAT THEY SAY ABOUT STUART BOWKER

"Great insight to how businesses work, and really interesting points"
Tony Gedge, Marketing Pirates of Dentistry

"I keep getting jewels of wisdom"
Kane Yeardley, Forum Bars Group

"Exactly what I need, this is gold dust"
Oliver Dax, Monkey's Paw Consultancy

"I didn't think of the marketing in that way- definitely something we can do to bring in extra profit"
Wayne and Carolyn Ewart, Skin and Health

"A unique ability to see the methods and systems that make others able to see how they can be successful too"
Mark Hopkins, Premier Event Bars

www.ingramcontent.com/pod-product-compliance
Lightning Source LLC
Chambersburg PA
CBHW071442180526
45170CB00001B/420